IN THE SILENCE OF RENEWAL
WE UNEARTH THE WHISPERS
OF A PURPOSE REBORN,
TURNING REJUVENTATION INTO
A LIGHT THAT GUIDES THROUGH SHADOWS.

M.C.Bell.

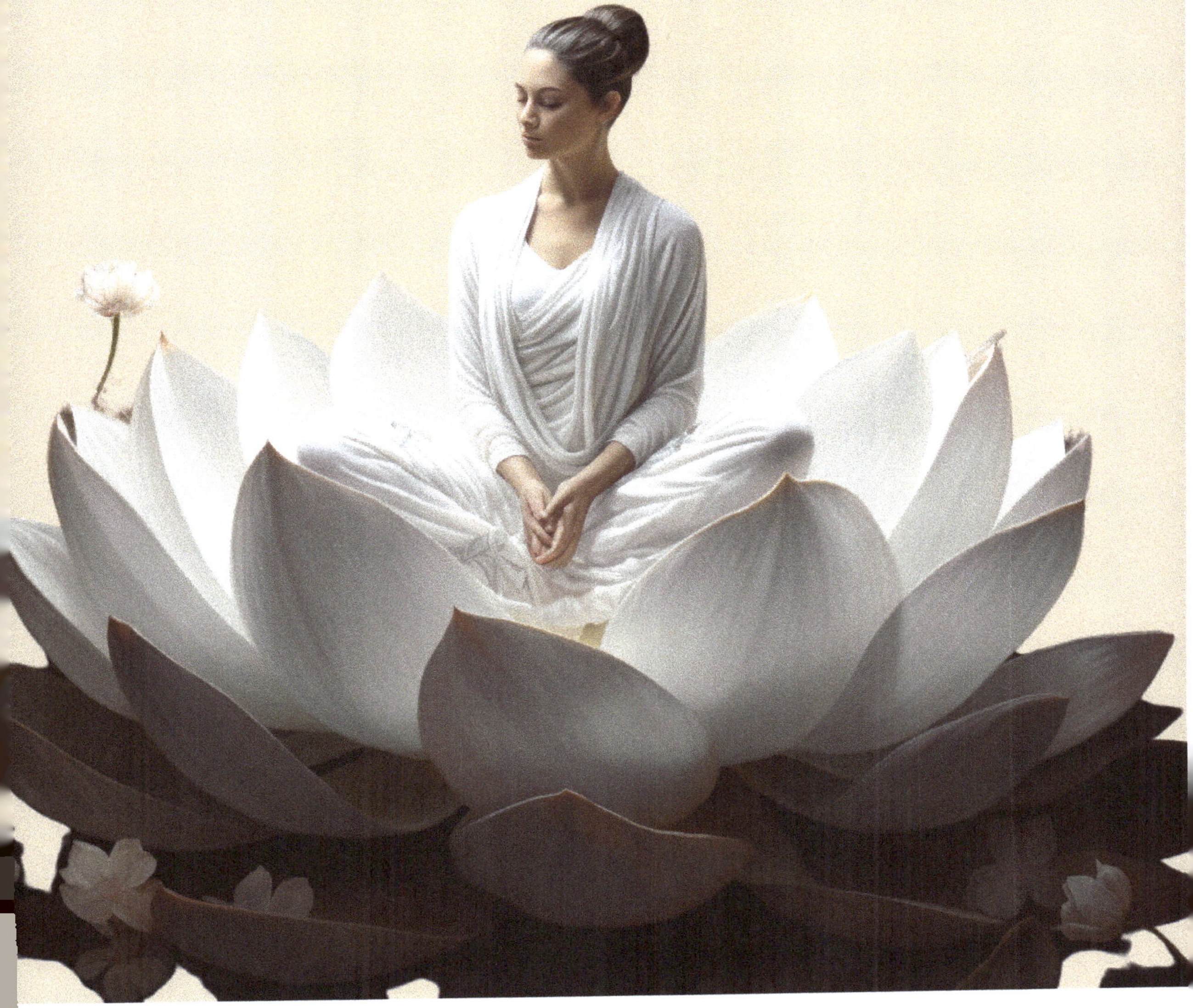

I've known Michele for nearly two decades, our bond forged during a profoundly challenging period—her son's battle with Bone Cancer. Witnessing her evolution through grief, marked by an incredible blend of strength and grace, has been both an honor and a deep source of inspiration for me. 'Rejuvenation' not only captures this journey from profound loss to healing but also crystallizes Michele's essence. It embodies the 'healing it forward' philosophy, a concept I hold dear and embody in my daily life.

This book, representative of her growth and the fourth stage of grief, resonates deeply with me, reflecting the transformative healing I've observed in her life. Her ability to convert personal adversity into a pathway for others' growth and rebirth is unparalleled. 'Rejuvenation,' alongside her other works, serves as a testament to the power of healing and the potential for renewal.

Supporting Michele's mission feels not just like a privilege but a celebration of the resilience and hope she embodies. Her narrative and initiatives, particularly through 'Rejuvenation,' inspire a healing journey that truly illustrates the essence of 'healing it forward.

– VIDA GUERRA Model + Actress

Foundation of
EMBRACE

Prelude to Stage Four

This foundational section provides a comprehensive overview of *The 7 Stages of Grief*, setting the stage for the deep dive into **REJUVENATE** that follows. While it serves as an introduction, it is designed to be revisited, offering insight and context as you navigate through each stage of your journey.

The EMBRACE Journey
Transform Grief and
Discover Inner *Strength*

Welcome, Warriors, to the extraordinary dimension of the 7 Stages of Grief Workbook Journal. I will guide you through a miraculous and empowering passage, unveiling the hidden treasures amidst the labyrinth of trauma and loss.

This course was born from my authentic desire to *heal it forward* in the grief community, ignited by theta meditation and a deep desire to manifest growth and healing through my writings. Drawing upon my intuitive theta-visions, I have created the EMBRACE framework — a radiant constellation of seven stages illuminating our transformative expedition in the wake of adversity.

In contrast to conventional approaches that merely skim the surface of emotions within the limited confines of the five stages of grief, I sensed the dire need for a holistic and transformative tapestry. The 7 stages of grief, meticulously crafted through my Healing it Forward modalities used in my 1:1 sacred retreats, transcend the ephemeral realm of emotions, ushering us into a realm where storytelling, the sacred utterance of our beloved's name, and the cultivation of gratitude mingle, guiding us through each challenging obstacle that graces our path.

Within this cherished community of kindred souls, we will unite, bound by a shared mission to collaborate, share our truth, and breathe life into one another's spirits—a sacred alchemy that fosters a radiant cascade of healing and metamorphosis. The modalities unveiled in the EMBRACE workbook journal's resplendent pages revolutionized how we navigate our sacred inner landscape, transforming the lives of those who have an unwavering longing to embrace the transformative work ahead.

As an extraordinary boon, I invite you to journey beside me as a Certified Grief Wellness Warrior, armed with the profound and purposeful modalities needed to extend a gentle hand to those ensnared in the clutches of their grief. By immersing yourself in these transformative practices and obtaining certification, you shall illuminate the path for others in their darkest moments, serving as a beacon of light and hope amidst the unfathomable abyss.

With deepest gratitude and genuine admiration, I extend my heartfelt appreciation to you for summoning the courage to embark upon the sacred journey of the EMBRACE workbook journal course. I assure you, Warriors, that this decision shall cascade with blessings and profoundly resonate. Together, let us traverse the infinite depths of grief, unlocking the wellspring of our inner fortitude and embarking upon a journey that transcends healing alone—a voyage brimming with purpose, renewal, and the willful power of the human spirit.

Prepare yourself for the transformational power of the 7 Stages of Grief Workbook Journal.

Let our extraordinary odyssey begin.

The Grief Warrior

Table of Contents

FOREWARD

My name is Cristal Sampson, and I work in mental health and psychiatry as a nurse practitioner in the UK, Connecticut, and New York, specializing in traumatic stress and mood disorders. I am also a young woman who experienced an early-term spontaneous miscarriage that burned a hole in depths I had previously not known existed. The revelation of this new depth of unconditional love, coupled with my baby's teeny heart stopping, left me hollow.

Even in my subsequent pregnancy the following year, I still felt empty of the unfulfillable desire for the baby back that I had lost in this life. The emptiness was filled with sadness, anxiety, and disappointment from troubled family dynamics – *a family unaware of my loss and grief.*

Someone with my expertise is never immune to the heartaches of the human experience, such as the loss of love and life. I recognized the potential to become an emotionally absent mother to my unborn baby, a fate that seemed all but certain at the time – and the thought terrified me. I am grateful to have understood that both my baby and I deserved the opportunity to heal. In my research, I discovered Michele, The Grief Warrior®.

As a health professional and a mental health specialist, I am particularly discerning about the services I opt for and the providers I choose. During this chapter of my life and given the circumstances, I did not pursue "traditional" mental health counseling. At that moment, confronting the challenges presented by contemporary therapy seemed beyond my capacity. I perceived the potential for a more conventional approach to be beneficial later in my healing journey.

What Michele provided touched the very core, breadth, and depth of my pain, reaching deep into the spiritual, mental, emotional, and energetic aspects of my being, body, and environment through a one-on-one retreat. I have not encountered anything like it since. Therefore, I am deeply moved that you are here, exploring the 7 Stages of Grief. Your journey with Michele's intentional energy, as conveyed through her books, and her custom human design modalities coupled with her healing energy, will extensively shift your essence and transform you.

FOREWARD

The 'EMBRACE: The 7 Stages of Grief' workbook series is designed to support every individual navigating grief—those who feel unprepared and overwhelmed by the complexities of losing a loved one. This series speaks to the heart of those oscillating between the anticipation of loss and the necessity of maintaining 'normalcy,' amidst the swirl of anger, resentment, and sorrow. It is a compassionate companion for every silent sufferer, for those caught in the emotional storm of impending loss, and for caregivers in dire need of nurturing themselves.

What distinguishes Michele's 'The 7 Stages of Grief' series most is the infusion of practical hope within its pages—a hope that is both tangible and deeply rooted in the natural spaces where resilience and healing begin. Michele brings a deep understanding and mastery in guiding others through the vast resources available for grief support, offering pathways that are both practical and easily navigable. Her insight into the caregiver journey, as a single mother is profoundly intimate, shaped by her own experience of lovingly supporting her teenage son, through his transition, enveloped in a cocoon of love. This unique perspective enriches her approach, making her guidance not only informed but deeply empathetic to the nuanced experiences of grief.

My work with Michele has caused a seismic shift in my perspective and has improved my relationships with myself, my family, and the people who meet me. I am moved with infinite gratitude at the positive and priceless impact my work with Michele has had on my experience of motherhood and the beautiful relationship my daughter and I get to have. Now, I enjoy expanding my connection as she has become a selfless friend and true mentor.

I encourage you to allow this book to transform you positively. Let it be a daily source of support and comfort, especially in moments of need. Remember, everything Michele has undertaken since Nicky's return to the Source has been a heartfelt ode to him and a homage to the enduring legacy of love and purpose he entrusted to her. Michele's ultimate wish is for you to discover your purpose and allow it to drive you forward through the cherished journey of your life.

Cristal Sampoon

FROM MY HEART
to yours...

Alignment in the face of loss is the only option. When we open ourselves to the possibilities presented to us, we find this harmony: in the strength of our words, in the peace of our meditations, in the gift of our presence, in the renewal of our bodies, in the stirring of our spirits, in the depth of our relationships, and in the nourishment we give ourselves.

The path to recovery is a beautiful tapestry that offers the opportunity for personal development and the forging of inner fortitude. We will brave new territory together, learn new things, and grow as people. I will be your guide and source of solace throughout our journey together. Get ready to reclaim your life with renewed confidence as you learn to swiftly navigate life's complications and unleash your remarkable inner potential.

There is nothing scary or complicated about this course since I will be there to guide you through every one of the steps. Let's take off on a journey into the unknown, where the payoff to SELF could be infinite.

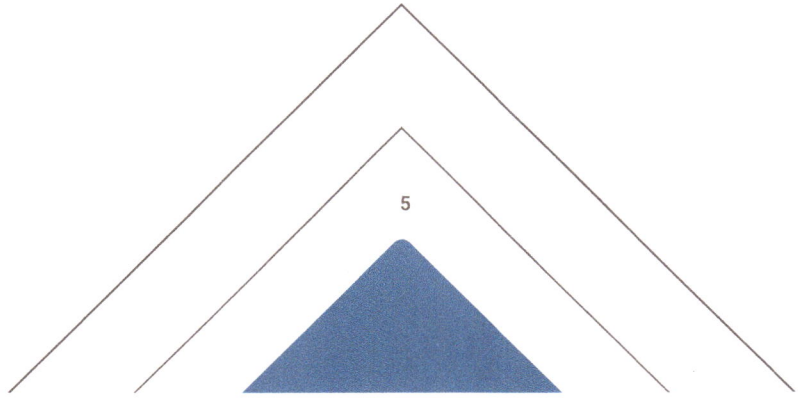

PROLONGED GRIEF DISORDER
Unveiled
as total B.S

Shattering the Illusion: Liberating Ourselves from the Constraints of the "5 Stages of Grief"

Adhering to established norms is a delusion, a fallacy we must quickly let go of when dealing with extended grief disorder. The "5 Stages of Bereavement" model developed by psychologists has been widely disseminated for too long, permeating every aspect of grief counseling and education.

Unfortunately, the constant push to conform to a set and narrow path of grieving has led me and countless other seekers within the grief community to feel disillusioned.

I beg you to disregard this erroneous advice immediately. The core meaning of our name, "EMBRACE," contains the whole truth. The concept of "Prolonged Grief Disorder" is 100% bogus.

The "5 Stages of Grief" concept originated from an unsupported theory meant to characterize the reaction of people who had been given fatal diagnoses rather than those who were navigating the maze of loss and sorrow. Here we have two utterly dissimilar yet actual experiences, each of which calls for special attention and comprehension.

6

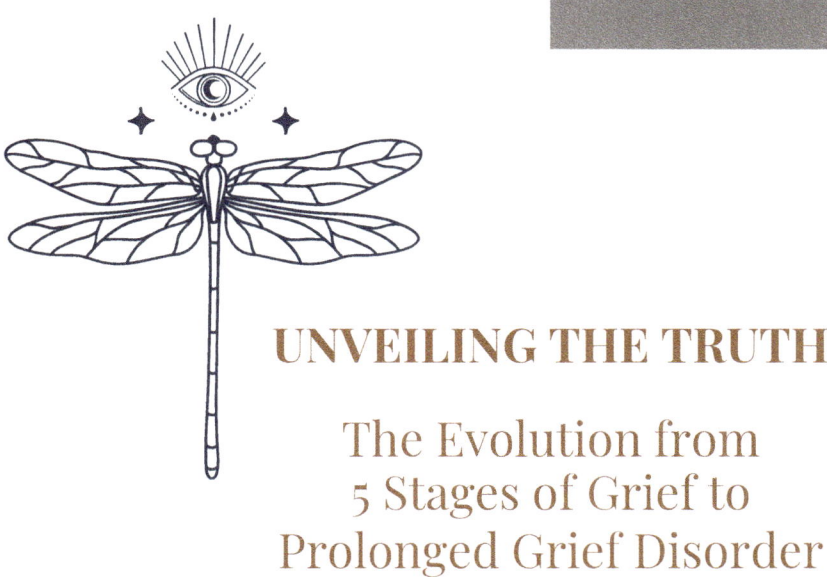

UNVEILING THE TRUTH

The Evolution from 5 Stages of Grief to Prolonged Grief Disorder

In March 2022, a new grief-related disorder was officially adopted into mainstream mental health diagnosis nomenclature. Seeing how the clinical world has further shamed the sacred grieving world is disheartening. DSM-5's trauma and stress-related category have a new label: Prolonged Grief Disorder, created deliberately to define what grief should and should not look like.

But first, let's take a moment to think. What exactly is this thing called "Prolonged Grief Disorder"? Claiming a year for adults and a paltry six months for children is an arrogant attempt to restrict the complex fabric of grief inside the confines of time. According to the American Psychological Association, persons who carry this label are assumed to exhibit the following symptoms even after the diagnostic window has closed:

- The crushing weight of grief pressed down on every aspect of their being.
- An unending fixation on sorrow as memories of the lost reverberate ceaselessly.
- A mental panorama obscured by agony or the unsettling absence of feeling.
- They engage in a delicate dance of denial and avoidance as they try to face their loved one's death.
- Dissonance and disconnection can develop when one feels different from the social norm.
- Every breath is filled with the haunting repercussions of despair and isolation.

We stand at the intersection of societal, cultural, and religious expectations, where the mere fulfillment of established criteria has become pivotal in making a prognosis. Understandably, when engulfed by the darkness of losing a loved one, such clinical classifications may not bring the peace and comprehension one wants.

To promote genuine healing, we need to permit ourselves to explore our inner emotional landscape freely.

Let us stand up as one in our resolve to overcome this stereotype's obstacles. Let us regain our freedom from societal norms to grieve and heal as we see fit.

We will overcome obstacles as a group and EMBRACE the journey of getting to the heart of our pain and reclaiming our ways forward in healing.

WHY PROLONGED GRIEF DISORDER
is Facing So Much Criticism

There is no moral compass in the arena of mourning.

Grief isn't reducible to a single feeling but incorporates many of them. It weaves a complex and ever-changing mosaic of emotions, including sadness, rage, anguish, loneliness, reverence, connection, and perplexity.

It's a shared adventure that everyone does on their terms.

Grief is complex and multifaceted: No two souls mourn alike, for no two losses are identical. Attempts to confine the grieving process within cookie-cutter stages, rigid criteria, and prescribed timelines propagate the fallacy of a right or wrong way to grieve.

Grief, in its essence, is a natural phenomenon—

A sacred dance that unfolds within the depths of our being. It is a deeply personal and profound experience, far from being a pathological problem to be solved.

A child's heart carries the imprint of a parent's absence for months or years. Similarly, a parent's longing for a child, partner, or loved one transcends all notions of time. The ache, the longing, lives in the very essence of our human nature.

Grief is an enigmatic path; Grief isn't linear.—

If we were to create a line graph of our grief journeys, it would be surprising for scientists to discover no discernible pattern.

Within the ebb and flow of our grief, we encounter good and bad days interwoven in a twisted dance.

Embracing this is how we move with our grief. Labeling and attempting to confine it only breeds resistance. Progress lies *not* in imposing a specific timeline but in surrendering to the ever-changing flow of our grief and learning to move on with acceptance and dignity.

Grief isn't inherently harmful.

Grief is evidence of love lost.

It serves as a poignant symbol of our love, our desire to cherish and remember those individuals and relationships that hold deep significance in our lives.

It's instinctively human: both beautiful and painful. By labeling grief as a problem in this sacred space, By labeling grief as a problem to solve, we carry it. By leaning into our pain, we *move with* it.

Grief looms of isolation. Support becomes our lifeline.

Grief defies measurement, transcending the confines of milestones as the 5 Stages of Grief imply. It is an ever-evolving journey, an ongoing experience. Pathologizing and diagnosing grief makes it feel abnormal. In reality, it represents so much of the human experience.

Diagnoses can empower us by illuminating how our minds or bodies function differently and offering solutions. However, diagnosing grief only deepens the shame, loneliness, and isolation. No one should feel wrong for grieving beyond a specific date.

We need grief support, not grief diagnosis. By creating space for its expression, allowing its capacity to unfold without restraint.

Unlock the Profound Power of Healing with EMBRACE
The 7 Stages of Grief Alignment

Are you prepared to immerse yourself on a journey of healing and self-discovery?

Step into a sphere of authenticity, truth, and love as you immerse yourself in the unparalleled wisdom and guidance offered in the transformative EMBRACE course. This course goes beyond the ordinary, offering a depth of healing that will leave an indelible impact.

What sets EMBRACE apart? It emerges from the heart of an expert grief practitioner, infused with the spirit of authenticity and infused by a genuine desire to empower and support individuals on their unique healing journeys.

EMBRACE offers a transformative approach that transcends traditional teachings.

Through this meticulously crafted course, you will unlock the tools and techniques to navigate the depths of grief, embracing healing and growth. The 7 Stages of Grief Alignment workbook becomes your trusted companion, providing compassionate guidance through each stage. It empowers you to honor your journey, embrace your emotions, and pave the way for a purposeful shift.

However, EMBRACE's path forward still needs to be completed. Those interested in learning more and becoming certified "Healing it Forward" practitioners will find that this course provides a beautiful opportunity to do just that. As a trained professional, you will be honored to assist others on their journey to wholeness and personal development.

The EMBRACE program is an astonishing journey of self-discovery and empowerment, not simply another healing class. It encourages you to look within, where you'll find the key to your inner wisdom and the key to your recovery. Along the journey, you'll be surrounded and transformed by a community of like-minded spirits who share your unyielding dedication to growth and give support and encouragement.

Are you prepared to take your life's most incredible life-changing healing journey? Join us on this life-altering adventure, where our north stars are sincerity, honesty, and love. Learn the true meaning of pivoting with intent through your experience with EMBRACE. Your healing journey awaits, and we are here to walk alongside you every step of the way.

Are You Ready?

ALL RIGHT, GRIEF WARRIORS:

We're breaking up with the 5 Stages of Grief

Meet your new boo,
the 7 Stages of Grief Alignment!

The 7 Stages of Grief Alignment knows no order. They are not steps but continual pillars, symbols, and actions to make space for grief in your growth.

Words hold immense power, and we choose to transform our grief rather than diagnose it.

The Grief Warrior

EMBRACE

THE 7 STAGES OF GRIEF ALIGNMENT

01

EXPRESS
Let your emotions guide you and experience the joy and fulfillment of expressing your true self through journaling and artistic exploration.

02

MEDITATE
Embrace the power of sitting with your grief, opening your heart, and leaning into the serenity of the present moment, creating space for healing and growth.

03

BE PRESENT
Pause. Observe and relinquish the need for constant busyness, and tune into the depths of your feelings. Embrace the beauty, opportunity, and purpose in this moment.

04

REJUVENATE
Reignite your zest for life, nourish your soul, and elevate your vibrations through the transformative power of self-care. Rediscover what it means to feel truly alive.

05

AWAKEN
Awaken the part of you that's been hiding. Reclaiming lost joy, energy, and vibrance. Rediscover the essence of your true self, waiting to be revealed.

06

CONNECT
Grief can separate us from true ourselves, making us feel like trapped observers of our lives. Reconnect physically, mentally, and spiritually to find your center and regain a sense of control and profound connection.

07

EAT HEALTHY
Nourish your body with the fuel it craves for strength and vitality. Embrace the sensory delight of flavors, textures, and intuitive connection as your body receives each healthy bite.

What 'stage' speaks to you?

IF YOU'RE READY TO TURN YOUR PAIN INTO FUEL...

Your past can lead you to your purpose.

Your pain can become your fuel to embody and fulfill that purpose. It's time to heal the resilient spirit within you, the one who has overcome more than imagined possible.

Unclench your jaw. Let out a sigh of relief - and stop running. We can't change our pasts. e may not alter our pasts, but we can find peace in our history and shape our futures by nurturing our souls in the present moment.

Each of us possesses a unique narrative shaped by our experiences. While we may not always have control over the plot, we have the power to choose the underlying theme. Let us craft our stories around the essence of healing rather than being defined by pain.

Rise as a warrior, not just a survivor. I am here to guide you because I believe in your strength.

It's time to take hold of the reins and chart a path toward healing, love, and inner strength.

i believe in you.

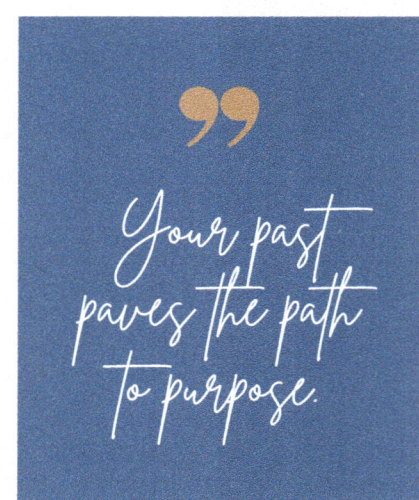

Your past paves the path to purpose.

Grab a pen, and we'll embark on your new journey together.

PIVOT *with* PURPOSE

My vocation is a sacred calling, where every word, line, and page is carefully crafted with intention and purpose. My vocation extends far beyond the conventional realms. It transcends the boundaries of traditional academia and ventures into the realm of energy and transcendence.

Having traversed the depths of deep trauma and loss, I intimately understand the weight of grief and despair. Yet, I alchemize that suffering into meaning through the art of writing, creating, and teaching. I am fueled by authentic and intentional love in every breath of my life.

It is not a love born out of obligation but a love that empowers and inspires, beckoning others to rise above their fears and embrace the limitless possibilities that lie within them.

To me, this is the very essence of sacredness.

Let this inspire you that, no matter your challenges, you can *Pivot with Purpose* and manifest life in alignment with your highest energy. As your Grief Warrior® mentor, I will guide you on a sacred transformation journey.

I HAD TWO CHOICES:
Retreat Or Renew

When my first-born son passed away, grief consumed me. I could have withdrawn from life, but a fire within me refused to give up. It was then that I realized grief is the expression of love. It's our mind and heart's way of grappling with loss. It requires embracing the unknown, for life itself is unpredictable, regardless of our beliefs.

In rediscovering the magic of life, I rekindled my commitment to live truly. The grief didn't vanish, but it became more manageable. I started noticing the small things that bring joy to life. Each day became an adventure filled with endless possibilities. With an open heart, I welcomed the uncertainties that came my way. While the aftermath of a loss can leave us feeling hopeless, the strength to persevere can lead to unexpected achievements. Withdrawing may seem tempting, but it only perpetuates a downward spiral. We can move forward and rediscover joy by renewing our commitment to purposeful living.

I crafted the 7 Stages of Grief Alignment to renew my commitment—a guide from eleven years of personal experience and introspection. My book, A Son's Gift, became a testament to living intentionally after unforeseen circumstances. This challenge navigates the unexpected tragedies that may befall us, particularly if we face intense grief for the first time. Each stage holds significance, and we must traverse them daily. It isn't always easy, but a life infused with meaning and purpose is worthwhile.

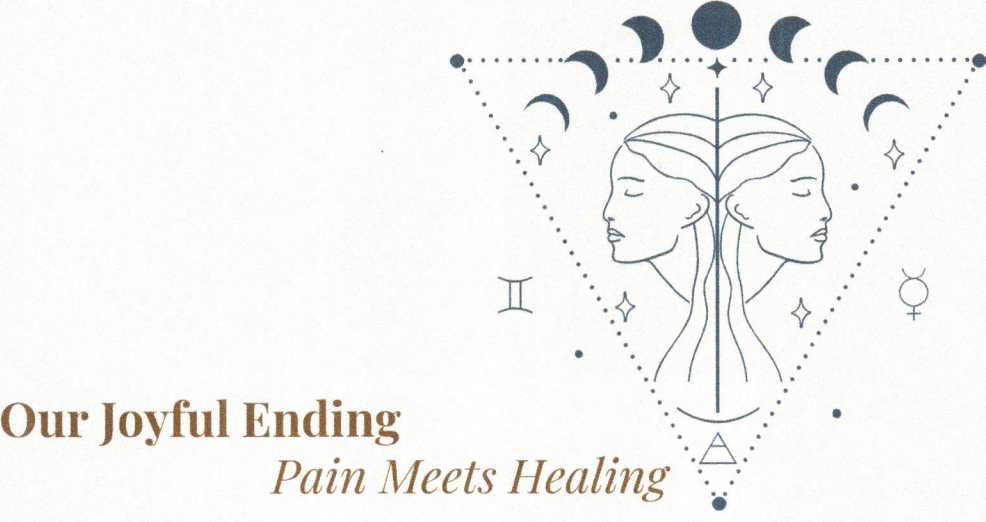

Our Joyful Ending
Pain Meets Healing

Once upon a time,

...in the whimsical land of Serenityville, a group of courageous warriors known as the Serene Seekers set forth on a remarkable quest—the Journey of Healing it Forward. Guided by the wise and enchanting fairy Seraphina, they discovered the secret power of acceptance. The goal was to align with the 7 Stages of Grief and release the mystical power inside.

The Serene Seekers set out on their journey full of bravery and love. As they wandered through enchanted forests and sparkling waterways, they experienced times of hardship. They didn't shy away since they knew the answer to their problems resided within themselves.

The Serene Seekers blazed a trail based on the ancient wisdom of the 7 Stages of Grief Alignment. Each phase—"Express," "Meditate," "Be Present," "Rejuvenate," "Awaken," "Connect," and "Eat Healthy"—held a vital piece of the puzzle to their recovery and development.

Under Seraphina's guidance, the Serene Seekers learned that pain was not their enemy but a teacher to be embraced. It became a part of their story, a testament to their courage and resilience. United in their journey, they supported one another, sharing stories and offering solace when needed. Their empathy and compassion wove a love web across Serenityville.

By embracing their pain, the Serene Seekers discovered the profound magic of healing it forward. They realized their healing could inspire and uplift others, spreading hope and resilience far and wide.

The Serene Seekers' journey through the 7 Stages of Grief Alignment showcased the power of acceptance and showed the world how beautiful it can be. Their travels exemplified the concept of "healing it forward," the idea that one person's kindness may positively impact others.

And so, the Serene Seekers continued their noble quest, fueled by determination and love. Together, they embarked on the Journey of Healing It Forward, embracing their pain, sharing their stories, and spreading seeds of healing throughout Serenityville and beyond.

This uplifting tale illustrates the power of facing our suffering and moving with "Healing it Forward."

HOW TO
Sit *with* Your Grief

ACKNOWLEDGE IT.

OWN IT.

EXPLORE IT.

THERE ARE 3 FUNDAMENTAL

STEPS TO EMBRACING YOUR GRIEF

FEEL *and*
ACKNOWLEDGE IT

Feel - Dive into the Depths of Emotion In the first step. We will learn the art of feeling. Relax your body and mind by closing your eyes and taking a few slow, deep breaths. Don't oppose or judge the feelings you're experiencing.

Are you on the verge of purging, overwhelmed by a storm of pain, guilt, shame, betrayal, or envy?

In EMBRACE, you will understand the depth of your pain through emotional exploration. Embracing our feelings shows respect for the integrity of our experience and lays the foundation for healing.

To *acknowledge* is to embrace the power of acceptance with the courage to feel. It is easy to dismiss our grief, burying it beneath layers of denial or self-judgment. But this step teaches us to embrace our pain by acknowledging its presence. Let go of the urge to push your feelings aside or berate yourself for struggling. Instead, recognize that grief is a natural and valid experience. When you own your suffering, you allow yourself the time and perspective to determine what's causing it.

OWN YOUR FEELINGS
of Pain, Grieving, Loss

Understanding your feelings is the first step, but owning your pain is crucial. Grief is often associated with a side of ourselves that we prefer to ignore, so we dismiss it. However, pushing your emotions aside or criticizing yourself for struggling can worsen things. Instead, it's essential to accept your pain as a natural and valid experience and take responsibility for it.

By holding yourself accountable, you can create the space and understanding necessary to delve deeper into the issue and uncover its root cause. This process of self-exploration allows you to work with your pain rather than fighting against it, leading to gradual healing and release from its grasp. With time, you may find that your pain becomes a source of wisdom and inspiration, helping you cultivate self-compassion, acceptance, and strength.

So, don't dismiss your pain or judge yourself for feeling it. Embrace it as an opportunity for self-discovery and growth, and let it guide you on your journey.

ARE YOU LIVING A LIFE *of Denial?*

Denial is a tempting refuge, an escape from facing the truth that awaits us. But is it truly living?

Yet, in denying our true selves, we rob life of its vibrant colors. We become sleepwalkers, traversing existence without truly seeing or experiencing its wonders. Disconnected from our emotions, we numb ourselves to the essence of our being, avoiding the aspects of life we dare not confront.

Grief has a way of leaving us feeling empty, disconnected from the world. Faced with such turbulent emotions, it is crucial to remain present. Opening ourselves to the surrounding reality allows us to reestablish our connection to ourselves and the world surrounding us.

If denial has become your shield for too long, it is time to confront the truth. Though it may be a painful pilgrimage, evading your emotions and sidestepping the obstacles that impede your growth will only perpetuate your suffering. To live a life of integrity and authenticity, we must be brave enough to acknowledge our wounds and fears.

Embrace the journey, for it may come with its share of challenges. Remember, transformation is not an overnight process; it requires time and intense dedication. But as you courageously confront your pain, you will uncover hidden wells of strength within. Say goodbye to denial and welcome the truth of your existence. With each intentional step, you carve a path toward a life filled with authenticity and purpose.

The path ahead may be arduous, but you are not alone. I am here to offer my unwavering support, accompanying you through every stride of this transformative journey. Embrace your inner resilience and have faith in the healing process.

Trust yourself and step boldly into a life of authenticity and growth. You have the power to rewrite your story.

The Guiding Light of *Embrace* Nurturing Those in Grief

Faced with another's grief, we often find ourselves at a loss for words. The profound pain and sorrow they bear can leave us powerless, uncertain of how to offer solace in their darkest hours. Yet, amidst the vastness of this challenge, there exists a flare of hope—a well-crafted grief book, EMBRACE.

In these pages, you'll find a companion journal that will bring comfort and understanding to those roaming the twisted path of sorrow.

While it is impossible to erase the pain, EMBRACE can soothe the aching heart and guide one's steps through the obstacles of grief.

The sentimental narratives make the emotions' kaleidoscope more explicit and the burden of grief more tolerable. As a treasured tool in your grief bag, the 7 Stages of Grief Alignment provides a roadmap for the griever and their companions, fostering awareness and healing.

Yet, it is crucial to remember that when supporting someone living in grief, the gift of your presence and enduring willingness to listen outweighs any words of wisdom or reassurance.

With its intricate nuances, grief often leaves those who mourn feeling isolated and misunderstood. EMBRACE is a heartfelt promise that assures you that you are not alone in your journey.

EMBRACE will offer hope and encouragement, reminding readers they are not alone in their sorrow. Consider giving them a copy to support a friend or loved one during grief.

If you want to support a friend or loved one during grief, consider giving them a copy of EMBRACE! You want the support of your loved ones, and the same goes for them needing you. As with any journey in life, the journey of grief as a team, we got this!

The Healing Dance of Grief
Nurturing the Spirit *within*

When someone close to us dies tragically, we are engulfed by an overwhelming sense of loss, accompanied by a symphony of painful emotions. We journey through this dimension of grief, uniquely navigating its twists and turns. Some shed tears like raindrops from a stormy sky, others ignite with fiery anger, while some retreat into the solitude of their inner world. These reactions, these expressions of grief, are the rivers that flow from the depths of our souls. We must honor them, for within these expressions lie the seeds of self-awareness and the catalysts for healing.

It's simple to feel disoriented and overwhelmed in today's fast-paced, ever-evolving society. The grieving process is a multifaceted test; we all long for the loving company of a compassionate that requires us to seek comfort from those who can relate. As a holistic practitioner, I stand ready with the tools and resources to accompany you on this sacred pilgrimage. Drawing upon my extensive experience, I offer a sanctuary where your voice can be heard, your story shared, and your healing ignited.

Discerning the way forward is exhausting in life's chaotic orchestra, where confusion and uncertainty reign. The weight of emotional pain may tempt us to forge ahead, mindlessly seeking an escape from the obstacles that hinder our progress. Yet, dear soul, a profound wellspring of resilience and strength lies within you. Developing spiritual growth can lead to a limitless abundance of peace and stability. Nurturing your connection with a higher power or the wisdom within you can help you navigate life's most brutal storms with grace and serenity. As you enter this sacred journey of spiritual expansion, you will uncover newfound capacities to navigate life's turbulent seas, supporting your passage and extending a loving hand to those who traverse similar paths.

The road may appear dimly lit as you tread its winding path. Yet, within you resides a radiance of faith, highlighting the darkness for those who desire comfort in your presence. Even when grief looms, keep hope alive in the sanctuary of your heart. I encourage optimism even in the darkness. Envision a shining star, your inner strength shining its light into the deepest crevices of despair. As you gaze upon the darkness, challenge fear and vulnerability to manifest and transform into a conduit for healing. By embracing the full spectrum of your being, shadows, and all, you control the destiny of self-empowerment. Even in the trenches of darkness, your intense light inspires and uplifts those who witness your strength and courage.

Remember that you are never alone in the sacred dance of grief, where each step is steeped with the essence of unconditional love. Reach out, Warrior, to those who can guide and support you on this transformative pilgrimage. Together, you will honor the pain, nurture your spirit, and spin a tapestry of healing that extends far beyond the realms of grief. Let the rhythm of your heart guide you, as it holds within it the tune of perseverance, the harmony of optimism, and the assurance of rejuvenation.

Shadows become tools that help shape Who You Are...

The Symphony of *Empathy* Navigating Responses to *Grief*

Why do some people run when I embrace my sadness?

Have you ever felt alone in your sadness because others choose to ignore or withdraw from you?

It's disheartening to question whether you deserve support or understanding. It can be challenging for those not accustomed to dealing with intense emotions like grief to face their feelings. Fear, unfamiliarity, and a lack of knowledge about responding supportively could all contribute to their feelings.

It can feel like others are trying to hide from the truth of your experience and being when they avoid hearing about your sorrowful tale. It might make you feel invisible, alone, and desperate for approval. An essential part of the grieving process is vulnerability, which searches for comfort in human connection and comprehension.

However, it is essential to note that only some can face and hold space for strong emotions, especially if they have not experienced something comparable. Their insecurity stems from a need for more ease with showing emotion. It's important not to take their reaction personally; instead, give yourself time and space to work through your feelings.

Be gentle with yourself and embrace the understanding that not everyone will comprehend or offer enduring support on this path. With time, you'll meet people who can hold the sacred space for your grief, opening doors to vital life lessons and opportunities for new relationships.

There can be many reasons why people don't respond to your melancholy expressions. Some people may struggle with displays of intense emotion, while others may feel ill-equipped to respond to someone who is deeply sorrowful. In certain instances, people may even fear that witnessing your sadness will awaken their dormant pain. It is essential to acknowledge that each person uniquely navigates grief, and adverse reactions to your sorrow do not show a lack of care or concern. Give them breathing room to deal with their feelings; they may discover the strength to help you.

As you continue your grief journey, remember that your emotions are valid and that your need for support is real. Seek solace in those who can hold space for your grief, and let go of the notion that everyone will understand. The dance of empathy requires patience and calls for self-compassion. If you care for yourself during this process, you show others how accepting melancholy can strengthen the spirit.

The Whispers of *Compassion*
Nurturing *Empathy* Through Small Acts

Empathy's complex webs of connection strengthen relationships during the grieving process. A kind touch, reassuring words, and a listening ear can go a long way toward alleviating emotional pain. During sadness, expressions of sympathy transform into a beautiful melody of support, kindness, and concern.

Even the tiniest gestures can convey the magnitude of affection and concern in moments of quiet reflection. Sincerity and love injected into the most straightforward actions can illuminate the darkest places. These seemingly insignificant acts go beyond words to bring solace to the soul. By doing these nice things for them, we can let them know they have our undying support and are not alone.

Sometimes, the answer lies not in words but in the silent embrace of companionship. To stand beside someone in their darkest hours to honor their wishes can transcend an act of compassion. You become a sanctuary of support for their wounded soul. Becoming a lifeline amidst the chaos by offering practical help, running errands, and preparing nourishing meals demonstrates that our warmth extends beyond mere words to sacred stillness.

They provide a sympathetic ear that accepts their suffering without judgment or making demands. We become instruments of compassion and wisdom, holding the door open for their recovery.

When words fail, being there and knowing how grateful we are can help comfort a broken spirit. Therefore, let us recognize the significance of greeting cards, reassuring embraces, and quiet moments of reflection. Aim to personify empathy, compassion, and concern. We become the vessels through which comfort is delivered, mending the broken parts of a mourning person's spirit in those quiet times.

You can use the following phrases:

My heart goes out to you; I'm sorry this is happening to you.
"What is your loved one's name?"
"What do you say we get some lunch together? Please tell me more about (insert name of cherished one here)."

The Unseen Language of Sorrow
Embracing *Understanding* and *Letting Go*

It's frustrating when those close to you don't understand how much your loss means to you. Some wonder if avoiding those who can't share our sorrow is right. But let's PAUSE to think about this:

No matter how well you articulate your pain, not everyone can comprehend complex emotions. Despite our efforts to articulate our pain, some may struggle to grasp its true essence. In these situations, letting go of our dependence on their comprehension is not a sign of a lack of strength or inability. Our efforts to help them understand the inexplicable would be well-spent.

Don't you think it's wonderful to imagine a world where empathy is cultivated and understanding becomes a part of our collective etiquette? While that ideal may be far off, we can take comfort in the company of those who share our values and offer proper understanding and support. Seek comfort in knowing you are not alone on your grief journey. By doing so, we create space for our healing, allowing our sorrow to unfold in its way, guided by our resilience and the support of those who truly understand.

01

Let us find comfort in the arms of those who truly understand and share our pain on this developing path of sorrow. Even if others can't understand our pain, it's reassuring that some would listen with empathy and provide a safe place to heal.

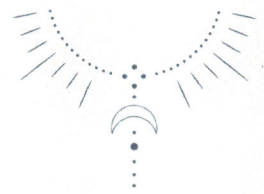

02

In the depths of sorrow, we are faced with a "griefosophical" lesson:

We are the chosen ones entrusted with the sacred duty of carrying the unseen language of sorrow. It is not a burden to bear but a calling that sets us apart from others. Our connection with our departed loved one runs deep, transcending the comprehension of others. The love we shared with them was unique, profound, and intimate, coloring our grief in hues that may mystify those who did not experience the same depth of connection.

Rather than harboring resentment or seeking understanding from those who cannot offer it, we can shift our perspective. It helps to think of ourselves as spiritual vessels that have solemnly promised to bear the burden of our grief. To mourn together is to witness the strength of love and reveal the depth of our connection.

By letting go of the expectation that everyone will understand our grief, we unlock a sense of communal understanding only discernible by our innermost beings. We become a collective source of higher consciousness. Our common grief language helps us bond with those who resonate with our vibe.

So, Warriors, Let up, hoping other people share your pain with you. Embrace the idea that you are connected to a group of people who "get it," and you become a force that cannot be stopped together. Make use of your suffering as a starting point for introspection and growth.

In doing so, you give tribute to the unconditional love you shared with your departed loved one and become that twinkle who walks this path of grief.

In grief, we are chosen to carry
the unseen language of sorrow,
a testament to our love and
resilience.

Unveiling the Art of
Respecting *Grief*

In this era of digital connectivity, we find ourselves conditioned to swiftly move on and brush aside the depths of our grief. Glossing over the importance of grieving and grief acceptance might be easy in today's fast-paced world. However, grief encompasses far more than prolonged sadness; it is an emotional journey that demands time, reverence, empathy, and patience to mend.

Loss, especially the irreparable loss of love, is at the heart of mourning. When we suffer a profound loss, it changes who we are and shines a light on what gives our lives true purpose. The path to recovery and growth lies in sincerely accepting our suffering.

Nobody enjoys being hurt, and most people will try to avoid it. However, suffering is a part of being human and must be faced head-on. Grief and loss, and the emotional sorrow they cause, are experiences all humans share at some point. Neither can we expect anybody else to take away our suffering, but we can show compassion, which can teach us a great deal about how to deal with the misery of others. Through compassion, we see that the suffering of others is natural and merits our whole attention.

The ability to empathize with others serves as a helpful reminder that there is no single "correct" way to deal with suffering. It is unnecessary to have all the solutions to be compassionate; all we need to do is be there for people when they are suffering.

So, when we see a loved one going through a tough time, let's not rush to ease their suffering. Instead, let's give our undivided attention to becoming wise. By doing so, we show them the kindness and consideration they deserve. There is an act of tremendous bravery, tenacity, and grit at the heart of mourning, an act that teaches profound truths about what it is to be human. So, let's not rush past the remembrances of limitless, unconditional LOVE.

Embracing the *Everlasting* **Journey**

BOTTOM *line*

One of life's greatest challenges is coming to terms with the fact that mourning is never really "done." We may reach a point where the raw pain of our loss has begun to fade, but the scars remain. These scars can be a source of strength and comfort. They remind us of the loved ones we have lost and help us appreciate life's fragility.

But keep in mind that you will never fully "get over" your loss. It is an ongoing journey that we all must travel. There may be days when the path is smooth and the going is rough. But eventually, we will reach our destination: a place where we can find peace and happiness again.

Healing is an ever-unfolding journey, an intricate dance of self-discovery and growth. As we set out on our journey, we recognize that our wounds are not who we are but a testament to our capacity to love fiercely and persevere through adversity. Unconditional self-love feeds the soul and opens the door to healing on all levels. Putting aside baggage and focusing on what brings us joy might help us find inner freedom.

You may find that your relationship with your loved one changes as you move through grief. Their presence becomes a source of strength and comfort, reminding you of their eternal love. You gradually rebuild your life as you heal, carrying their memory within you. Their spirit entwines with yours, illuminating the path to a meaningful existence.

While healing may never be complete, grief can propel you toward a more positive emotional journey. Embracing and expressing your grief healthily allows for soul healing to begin.

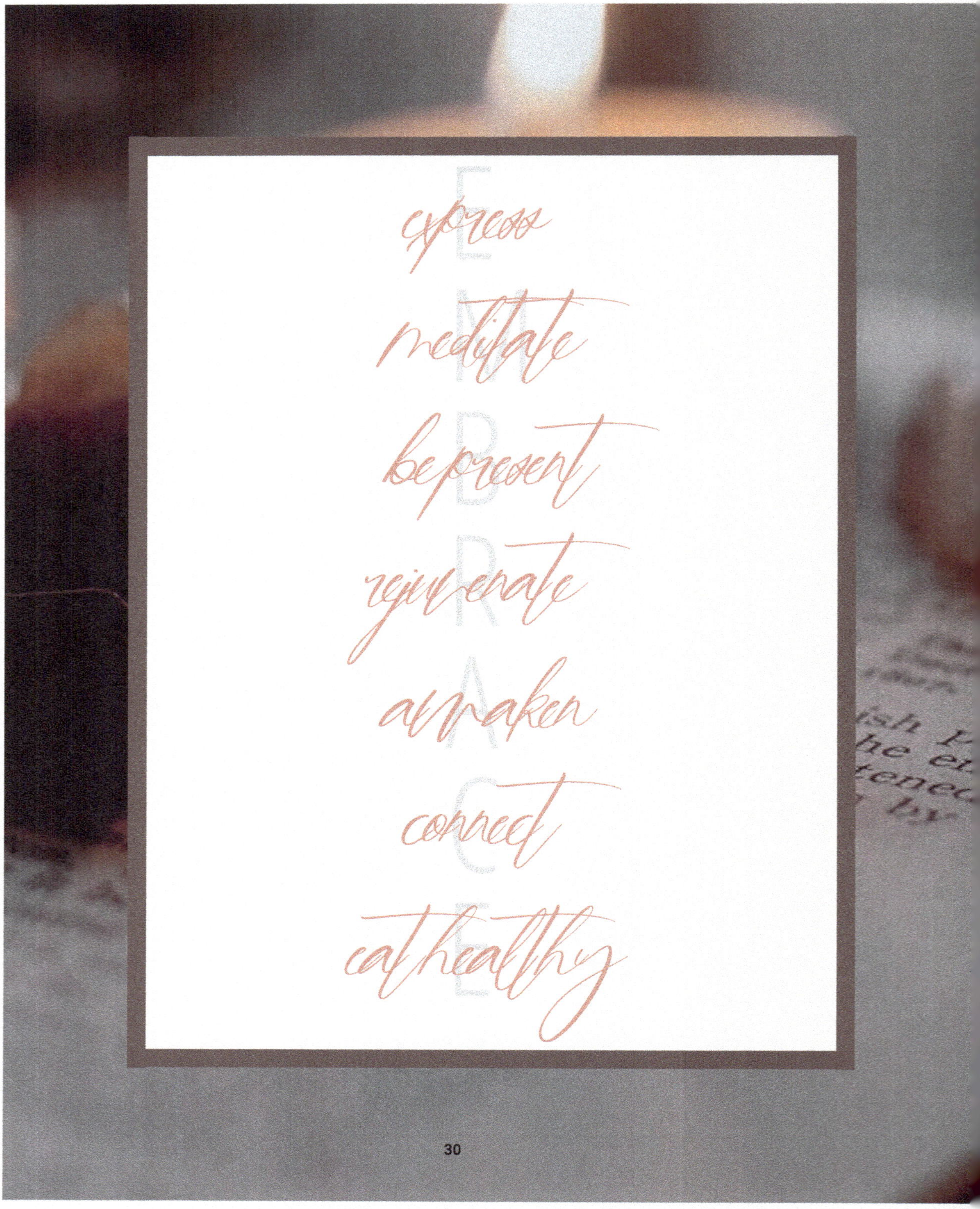
EMBRACE
express
meditate
be present
rejuvenate
awaken
connect
eat healthy

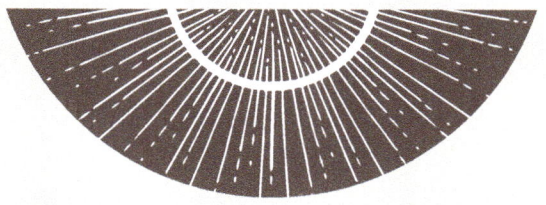

DOES EMBRACE
Speak to You?

Explore the transformative power of The 7 Stages of GRIEF Alignment workbook journal, designed to support you authentically and effectively on your grief journey. Each stage of this journal is carefully crafted to nurture your physical and mental well-being, empowering you to strengthen critical aspects of your health as you navigate through the aftermath of a traumatic event. Embracing these stages will lead you to greater strength, resilience, and a revitalized sense of purpose.

Drawing from personal experiences of loss and trauma, I created the 7 Stages of GRIEF Alignment mini journal to assist those willing to EMBRACE in their healing process. Within its pages, you'll discover practices that have deeply impacted my grief journey, enabling me to navigate through the pain and embrace genuine growth mindfully. These practices have brought about timeless healing, from releasing old attachments to rebuilding a lost sense of unconditional love.

This eternal healing perfectly captures the beauty of "Healing."

Whether at the beginning of your grief journey or making progress, embracing the stages outlined in this journal can ease the burden and infuse joy into your life. Let's say you've had enough and are ready to start living again. Please join me on the 7 Stages of the GRIEF Alignment workbook journal's transformational journey, or go even further and earn your Certified Wellness Warrior designation.

Take a deep breath, stay resilient, and remember that even in the darkest moments, we possess the inner strength to move forward. Embrace this opportunity and witness its profound impact on your life. Not doing so would be a mistake.

EXPRESS

Welcome to the First Stage of Grief Alignment: Express. In this stage, we encourage you to unleash your thoughts, feelings, and trauma through emotional journaling. By embracing this practice, you voice your emotions and release anxiety, triggers, and pain.

Reflect on its meaning in your grief journey and explore its significance. Use your notebook as a place of refuge where you may explore who you are and how you got here. Allow your own words to heal and shape your spirit.

Three ways you can integrate 'Express' into your daily therapy:

Emotional Journaling
Write freely each day to express and process your emotions.

Artistic Expression
Engage in creative activities to communicate and release emotions.

Verbal Communication
Share your feelings with a trusted person or practitioner for support and validation.

Expression is the key to unlocking our connection, allowing us to co-create a reality rooted in love and acceptance. So say their name, share your story, feel every moment, and remember—you are here for a reason. And always remember—you are here with a purpose. You have the power to create. So keep expressing yourself—you have everything it takes to thrive!

How will you express today?

MEDITATE

Have you ever explored the richness of meditation? It offers a gateway to discovering tranquility and clarity in grief or challenging moments. By dedicating time to cultivating mindful awareness, we unlock the potential for remarkable revelations.
With each intentional inhalation and exhalation, we create a sacred space within ourselves, allowing us to confront our emotions from a higher perspective.

Discover peace in nature's embrace, where meditation unveils transformative insights.

Pause for a moment and ask yourself: When was the last time you truly paused and immersed yourself in the vivid reality of "here"? It is in the here and now, the ever-present moment, where true existence lives. It is within this moment that the miracle of life unfolds.

BE PRESENT

'Be Present' is the 3rd Stage of Grief Alignment, encouraging us to be still. Society often expects us to conform to specific standards, but we have the power to within ourselves begin a path toward wellness simply by showing up.

Being present allows us to reconnect with life, love, and feel again.

Let's focus on being present and mindful. Pay attention to your breath - feel the rise and fall of your chest and let it move like a symphony's crescendo. Focus on the present and feel the caress of each inhale and exhale. Take in the vibrant feelings that sweep your entire being, and let them merge with the present moment.

Allowing your emotions to take over can be liberating. Accepting and working with our feelings without hesitation or judgment is crucial. Whatever those emotions may be, it's okay to feel them. Take a moment to permit yourself to step back, allowing your soul to have time within this very breath.

REJUVENATE

For true revitalization, we must turn inward and examine our bodily, mental, and spiritual states.

It can help us reclaim our vitality and lead us toward joy and fulfillment, especially when dealing with the loss of a loved one or the constant stresses of modern life. Transformation comes with self-reflection, inner growth, and healing. You have the power to do this!

By embracing new challenges and striving to grow in every aspect of our lives, we can reignite the spark and fire up our souls. So, why wait? We can rejuvenate and awaken joy at every level with determination and self-acceptance.

Reflecting on our loved ones and the gifts they gave us can also help rejuvenate our lives in their honor. Whether remembering a favorite memory or reaching out to those who supported us during difficult times, each act deepens the connection between us and our loved ones, even as they move beyond the physical world.

Ultimately, we choose how to react to grief, but by acknowledging our journey and embracing joy, we can find strength in our spirit again.

AWAKEN

In the 5th Stage of Grief Alignment, Awaken, you are invited to embrace the essence of being fully alive and anchored in the present moment. Retaining and shielding ourselves from raw emotions and harsh realities is expected in the depths of grief.

Awakening is the key that unlocks the door to our inner resilience and rekindles our faith in the truth that lies before us.

Pause and contemplate your life as it stands today. Allow this fresh perspective to offer a broader view, enabling you to observe your journey from a distance. In this introspection, you may realize that all you need lives within, and a vast expanse of possibilities awaits you on the horizon.

Let's embrace the awakening, as it acts as a catalyst that propels us forward with a renewed sense of vitality and purpose on our journey.

CONNECT

In the 'C' of EMBRACE, we find the power of connection in the 6th Stage of Grief. As we make our way through the complexities of this world, now is the moment to strengthen our connection to ourselves, our spirit, and our mind. While it may pose challenges, remember that we all thrive on daily connections.

How will you choose to CONNECT today?

Your mind. Your body. Your spirit.

Make a conscious effort to connect with yourself by dedicating just five minutes to express gratitude, a walk in nature, engaging in reflective journaling, cooking, creating, or allowing yourself to be still. Focus on self-care and self-reflection to enhance your well-being.

Tune in to your needs and honor them, for it is in these connections that true healing and growth can flourish.

EAT HEALTHY

In the final stage of our grief alignment journey, we are called to embrace the importance of nourishing ourselves through healthy eating. As we have journeyed through the different stages of grief in our course, we have learned the significance of addressing our emotional, mental, and spiritual needs. Now, we focus on the physical aspect of our well-being, recognizing that what we put into our bodies directly impacts our healing process.

Eating healthy becomes the inner thread that weaves all the stages of our grief alignment journey. By nourishing ourselves with wholesome, nutrient-rich foods, we provide our bodies with the fuel to support our healing from the inside out. We actively participate in our healing process by prioritizing foods promoting strength, vitality, and well-being.

As we continue our journey beyond grief, let us carry healthy eating lessons. Let us embrace the power of wholesome foods to support our ongoing healing and growth.

It is through this holistic approach that we can truly thrive and create a life that is vibrant, nourished, and filled with joy.

YOUR INNER
spiritual warrior!

EMBRACE is the ultimate exhilarating journey of healing and transformation. This course is not just a certification—it is a profound commitment to healing and a powerful dedication to moving forward with purpose.

We encounter countless challenges that test our resilience and tempt us to give up. Yet, deep within us lies an untapped well of strength, waiting patiently to be discovered and unleashed. This course empowers you to tap into that inner strength, unlock your full potential, and become the vessel to *healing it forward*.

The key lies in listening to your heart and trusting your instincts. By tuning into the untapped wisdom at the core of your being, you gain the clarity and guidance needed to navigate any obstacle that comes your way. With a resilient focus, you cultivate the courage and determination required to ***move with*** emotional barriers.

As you EMBRACE this journey, you discover that nurturing your inner world positively impacts your external world, cultivating meaningful connections with others, and investing in your self-enlightenment. The key lies in listening to your heart and trusting your instincts.

The 7 Stages of Grief Alignment will be your guiding light as you EMBRACE each stage of grief in your own time. Recognize that these stages are not linear processes; you may move back and forth between them as you navigate your unique grief journey. This flexibility allows you to honor your experience and progress at your own pace.

Are you ready to step into your power as a Certified Grief Wellness Coach?
Sign up today and trust your inner calling, take that leap of faith, and let your guiding light illuminate the path of healing and transformation for yourself and others.

A Graceful Pivot to Purpose

you've made it

You are now ready to **EMBRACE** our fourth Stage:

rejuvenate

That's the blessing and power of **pivoting with purpose.**

What are the 7 Stages of Grief Alignment?
Express. **M**editate.
Be Present. **R**ejuvenate.
Awaken. **C**onnect. **E**at Healthy.

Healing begins with acceptance and alignment transforms
us through embracing our circumstances.

**The empower of embracing is in your next chapter –
are you ready to turn the page?**

Table of Contents

Discovering What Rejuvenation Means For You

OBJECTIVE:

To create your definition of rejuvenation,
discover what makes you feel most excited
about life, and let it rejuvenate your soul!

A Note of Love:
What Does it Mean to Rejuvenate?

No grief journey is the same. So why are we still treating them like they are?

No more following the outdated 5 Stages of Grief or cookie-cutter methods. Your story is yours, and it's your turn to write the next chapter.

This one's going to be fun! Together, we'll relax, recharge, and (you guessed it) rejuvenate. You might think, "But Michele, what does that mean?"

If you ask the dictionary, it'll tell you that to rejuvenate is:

"To make young or youthful again."

"Give new vigor to."

"To restore to an original or new state."

But since you're the author of this journey, it's up to you to write your definition of rejuvenation!

For me, it's the harmony of the old and new. Paying tribute to the past and embracing the present is what it is. It's like feeling alive and excited about life again! It's reconnecting, envisioning my best life, going on spontaneous trips, practicing self-care, tuning into my divinity, and simply finding restoration in every deep breath.

Rejuvenation may hit you like lightning. Or, a slow, steady sun might fuel your soul and start your next chapter—rise, gradually spreading light and energy on what's right before you. A reset button that wakes you up.

It's time to start living. It's time to unwind. It's time to rejuvenate.

Journal Prompts
What does rejuvenate mean to me?

Reflect on your unique grief journey: What aspects set your experience apart from others?

_____

_____

_____

_____

Define your version of rejuvenation. What does it mean to "feel most alive and excited about life"? Be the author of your rejuvenation story!

_____

_____

_____

_____

Harmonize the past and present: How can you pay tribute to your past while fully embracing the present?

_____

_____

_____

_____

_____

What small step can you take today to begin embracing the power of rejuvenation in your life?

_____

_____

_____

_____

_____

_____

Journal Prompts
What does rejuvenate mean to me?

When I think of rejuvenation, what images or feelings come to mind?

Take a moment to visualize what it means to you personally.

_____
_____
_____
_____
_____
_____

Reflect on a time when you felt completely rejuvenated. What activities or experiences led to that feeling?

How can you incorporate more of those elements into your life?

_____
_____
_____
_____
_____
_____

Consider any obstacles or barriers preventing you from experiencing rejuvenation in your life.

How can you overcome these challenges and create space for rejuvenation to thrive?

_____
_____
_____
_____
_____
_____

Exercise

- Choose an environment, term, or action from your journal prompt responses. How could you make it a reality in your daily life?

- Consider yourself energized by activities that delight you, such as going to your favorite park, listening to motivating music, or engaging in self-care.

- Envision an intense beam of light flooding your being with a new sense of optimism and strength. Imagine the appearance and sensation of the light - it could be any hue you prefer. It may be warm, cool, or empowering.

- Allow this light to guide you in your quest for rejuvenation. Let it infuse your being like a tranquil sunrise or a powerful lightning bolt.

- Take some time to describe the energizing light that you are currently feeling. Try to be detailed and let your creative side flow freely. This description will help you to remember this feeling in the future, whether you do something rejuvenating or visualize the light filling your soul. Let yourself have some fun with it!

Creating a New
Way to Navigate

OBJECTIVE:

To map out your current grief navigation and reroute it toward growth, healing, and purpose.

A Note of Love:
How Are You Currently Navigating Your Grief?

Why not take a different route and allow the fresh air to rejuvenate your spirit? Breaking out of your routine is crucial for your well-being.

The grieving process is not just a momentary interruption or a solitary occurrence.

It is an entirely new course and direction in our existence, and we need a different way of navigating this unfamiliar territory.

Assessing your current place on the journey is critical to navigating your grief process effectively.

How are you coping with your loss? Is it actively influencing you, or is it directing you? Or do you let it rule you? Let's have an open discussion about it.

I assure you there are no right or wrong answers, only the need for honesty and self-awareness.

Allow time and space to process sadness. Reflecting on emotions can improve understanding and emotion management.

It's easy to run out of fuel on this journey, to become fatigued, exhausted, and feel like giving up on trying to move forward for weeks, months, or even years.

But I'm here to remind you to fill your tank. Fill your cup. Find a rest stop, take a deep breath, and give yourself a break.

You deserve it. Period!

Journal Prompts
What does rejuvenate mean to me?

How can you break out of your routine and infuse your days with new experiences that nourish your well-being?

_____

_____

_____

_____

Where are you on this journey, and how can you navigate this unfamiliar territory with self-compassion and understanding?

_____

_____

_____

_____

Assess how your loss is influencing you. Is it actively guiding your actions, or do you feel overwhelmed by its direction?

_____

_____

_____

_____

_____

_____

Reflect on your emotions and explore their depths to understand better and manage them. How can you create a safe and nurturing space for this emotional journey?

_____

_____

_____

_____

_____

_____

Exercise

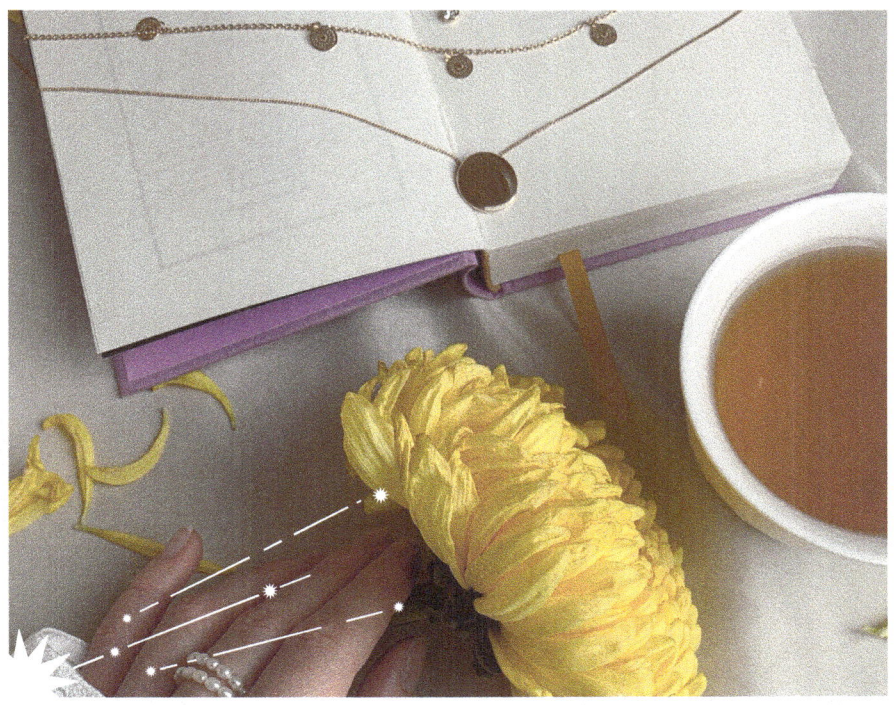

- Reflect on your journey through grief, noting the significant moments and emotions you have experienced.

- Identify the stages of grief you have encountered, disregarding the limitations of the traditional '5 Stages of Grief.'

- How has each one shaped and transformed you and helped you embrace the uniqueness of your grief process?

- Use your insights to create a personalized map of your grief journey, honoring your path of healing and growth.

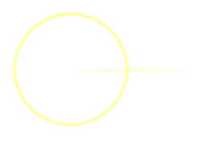

A Note of Love:
Create a New Path of Navigation

You know where you are now, which leads us to the question:

Where do you want to be?

When navigating your grief, there's no right way to approach it. Whether finding a hidden path, creating a secret tunnel, or taking a scenic route, options are available. What's important is figuring out how you want the experience to feel and look. Remember, you have the power to reroute your journey through grief.

It's important to follow your heart and pursue what you truly desire. There's no need to hold on to sadness and view it as a burden, a curse, or a punishment.

Consider using the 7 Stages as a guide. Transform your discomfort into significance by focusing on what you need right now.

Discover a new route for navigation that revitalizes and refreshes you. A path that allows you to rest, mourn, grieve, and savor all at once.

That's what our angels want for us. That's what your angel wants for you. May they guide and lift you to your new journey ahead.

Journal Prompts

Where do you envision yourself on your grief journey, and what steps can you take to navigate toward that destination with purpose and intention?

_____
_____
_____

How can you embrace the freedom to choose your path through grief, discover hidden routes, create new ones, or take a scenic and healing approach?

_____
_____
_____

What desires and aspirations in your heart can propel you forward, empowering you to let go of burdensome emotions and embrace the transformative power of grief?

_____
_____
_____

How can you use the 7 Stages to find significance and growth within discomfort, allowing you to focus on what you need for healing?

_____
_____
_____

In your quest for a revitalizing and refreshing route, how can you create space to rest, mourn, grieve, and savor all the different aspects of your experience, honoring the guidance of your angels on this new path of discovery?

_____
_____
_____

Vision Board Exercise

Incorporate these prompts into your vision board. The vision board serves as a daily reminder of the path you want to take, helping to keep you focused, motivated, and aligned with your intentions for healing and growth.

- Envision Your Destination: Imagine where you want to be on your grief journey.

- Explore New Paths: Discover alternative ways to navigate grief and find solace.

- Follow Your Heart: Pursue joy and healing without holding on to sadness.

- Design Your Route: Create a personalized roadmap for healing and self-care.

Honoring Our Loved Ones

OBJECTIVE:

To explore the power of not just moving with
your grief but leaping forward with it!

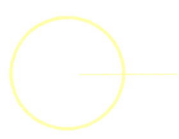

A Note of Love:
Leaping Into Your Next Level

We've talked all about moving with your grief. But let's not stop there.

One of the most rejuvenating ways to honor your loved one is by living your life to the fullest. Pursue your dreams, take action, and accomplish that one thing you always discussed with them. Let your love for your angel fuel a new passion.

Grief has the potential to awaken us if we let it. It reminds us of what is truly important and can provide us with clarity, emotions, and spiritual guidance to assist us in rejuvenating.

For you, that jump could mean launching the business you've always wanted to start. Perhaps it's mentoring, coaching, or assisting someone in your circumstance. Relocating to the beach, the country, or the city

Writing a book, buying a house, or taking that dream vacation.
Or maybe it's starting therapy and prioritizing self-care.

You know, that next-level version of you. Honor your loved ones by leaping to the next level in their honor!

Do something outside the box. Do something you'd never considered before—your next level is waiting!

Journal Prompts

What dream have you always shared with your loved one, and how can you take action to pursue it now, letting their love fuel your passion?

_____

_____

_____

Grief has the potential to awaken us to what truly matters; what newfound clarity, emotion, or spiritual guidance can you use to rejuvenate and take a leap forward in your life?

_____

_____

Think about the possibilities: launching that long-dreamed business, mentoring others, moving to a new place, writing a book, or taking a dream vacation - which next-level leap feels right for you to honor your loved one's memory?

_____

_____

_____

Challenge yourself to do something bold and out of the box, something you'd never considered before; what action can you take to leap to the next level and embrace the life that honors your loved one powerfully?

_____

_____

_____

Vision Board
Exercise

- Gather magazines, images, and quotes representing the 'next-level' version of yourself and the life you want to live in honor of your loved one.

- Select pictures that inspire you to start your mornings with joy, embrace each day with purpose, and infuse your daily life with passion and fulfillment.

- Include visuals that symbolize the kind of work you want to do, whether starting a business, mentoring others, or pursuing a career that brings you fulfillment.

- Find images that depict how you envision your rest and play, whether traveling to new places, enjoying hobbies, or spending quality time with loved ones.

- Choose pictures representing the type of place you want to live, whether it's a peaceful countryside retreat, a bustling city apartment, or a cozy beachside home.

- Assemble the images, quotes, and visuals on a vision board, arranging them in a way that sparks joy and inspiration. Display your vision board in a place where you can see it daily, allowing it to remind you of the leap you're taking to live your life to the fullest in honor of your loved one.

A Note of Love:
Explore the World to Explore Your World

In the last chapter, we mapped out your new grief navigation. Now, it's time to head to a destination unknown!

Traveling is one of the most powerful ways to shift to your next level. You are traveling, intending to leap!

Remember: We're not just moving with your grief. We're taking a leap you've never thought of before.

For example, you might do something or go somewhere your loved one would never imagine you doing but would be amazed and inspired to see.

Going to Coachella. Reigniting your magic in the Sedona desert, sinking into the Canary Islands sand, exploring the quiet of the Colorado mountains, or finding yourself in the city's vibrance.

Have you ever traveled to a destination in sync with your desired energy? This is where the healing begins for all my grief warriors.

This is why I offer 1:1 retreats: Destination Unknown. These leaps form a transformative path for warriors to explore themselves. It's mystically explosive, whether recovering from loss, trauma, suicide, or abuse.

What a JOY it would be to revitalize our healing spirits!

Journal Prompts

Have you ever imagined yourself in a destination that perfectly aligns with your desired energy? A place where you feel connected to your loved one's spirit?
Where will your leap of healing take you?

_____
_____
_____

What bold step can you take to honor your loved one and inspire yourself? Embrace the unknown and discover new possibilities on your journey.

_____
_____
_____

Are you ready to revitalize your healing spirit? What does a "Destination Unknown" retreat look like to you? (location, days, season, theme)

_____
_____
_____

Honoring Our Emotions

OBJECTIVE:

To honor our emotions by embracing the present, permitting ourselves to rest, and discovering a new perspective.

A Note of Love:
Giving Your Emotions Permission to Just... Exist!

Lack of motivation has nothing to do with having poor days or experiencing uncomfortable feelings. Our resilience in the face of pain's how we cope when things go wrong.

Feelings can't be judged as "good" or "bad." Feeling and healing through emotions does not need you to convince yourself there is a "right" or "wrong" way to feel.

Because they are uniquely yours, only you can adequately respect your feelings. I will not try to persuade you there is one way to improve.

But I will tell you that we recover more quickly when celebrating rather than punishing our feelings. We may provide the solace and care they require by welcoming and accommodating them.

Giving yourself to your feelings gives you the strength and insight to decide whether to let them in or out. Allow your sadness to be there. It is good, from a few weeks to several years.

Allow yourself to relax and give up fighting. Renew. Rejuvenate. Consider it your "emotional PTO" (Paid Time Off). Stop with the forced laughter and "should ofs."

Be Present.

Journal Prompts

How do you typically react to your bad days and painful emotions? Reflect on your immediate responses and whether they involve resistance or acceptance.

_____

_____

_____

Are there any emotions you tend to suppress or judge as "bad"? Why do you think you react this way, and how might it affect your well-being?

_____

_____

_____

Imagine giving yourself emotional PTO (Paid Time Off) to resist your feelings. Think about a recent challenging experience or a "poor day." How did you cope with it and show compassion during that time?

_____

_____

_____

Exercise

- Take some time to locate a serene spot and explore your emotional terrain.

- Visualize your feelings as weather patterns: storms, fog, clouds, sunshine, rainbows, snowfall, or winds. Recognize that these emotions are neither good nor bad –– check in with your emotional weather report.

- Now, instead of trying to alter the weather, envision yourself donning rain boots and stepping outside. Embrace the clouds' shapes, the fog's enigma, or the comfort in the cold.

- Adapt and flow with the emotional weather you're experiencing rather than pushing against it. Allow yourself to adjust and find the beauty in each emotional climate.

A Note of Love:
Honoring Your Grief Emotions in a New Light

There are beautiful ways to honor every shade, shape, and sheen of emotion. There is something magical about honoring your grief in a new light rather than alone in the dark. Again, there is no right or wrong way, but I hope you can look at it in a new light today.

However, you're feeling. Happy or sad. Angry or annoyed. Hopeful or confused. It's valid –– and I want you to see that more rejuvenatingly.

Channel that emotion of writing a poem, starting a painting, or creating something new!

Do something you and your angel loved to do together. Listen to their favorite music, read their favorite book, or watch their favorite movie! Look at pictures or share your favorite stories about them.

- Go for a walk, or spend a relaxing day inside!
- Honor an old tradition, or start a new one!
- Take a day for yourself, or reach out to old and new friends and loved ones!

There is no right or wrong –– only what's right for you. Connect your grief emotion, whatever it may be, and honor yourself with it.

Emotions mean you care. Caring is often painful –– but I promise, it's one of the most magical things about you. Let your magic rejuvenate your soul.

Journal Prompts

Reflect on a recent emotional experience you had. How did you initially respond to it, and did you feel comfortable embracing that emotion? If not, explore why and how you can honor it moving forward.

_____
_____
_____

Think about a creative outlet that appeals to you (e.g., writing, painting, or crafting). How might you use this outlet to channel and express your emotions in a healing and transformative way?

_____
_____
_____

Recall a cherished memory with your loved one. How can you incorporate elements of that memory into your present life to honor their presence and keep their spirit alive?

_____
_____
_____

Exercise

Create an Emotion Magic Board: On a piece of paper or in a journal, create a visual representation of your emotions using colors, shapes, and words. Each emotion can have its section on the board. As you experience different emotions, add to your magic board to acknowledge and embrace them. Use this board as a reminder that all your emotions are valid and contribute to the beautiful tapestry of your being. Allow your emotions to guide and inspire you with compassion and love as you move through the grief journey.

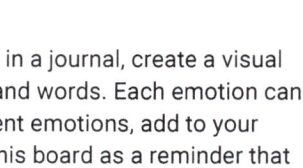

Kicking Up Your Serotonin

OBJECTIVE:

To understand how you can care for your
brain to rejuvenate your body and soul!

A Note of Love:
Give Yourself a Mental Health Boost!

We've mapped out your new grief navigation and envisioned your destination unknown... Now, it's time to fuel your soul for the journey!

Our brains are an ongoing science experiment of chemicals, neurotransmitters, and hormones. Knowing how your brain works can rewire, refuel, and rejuvenate it with excitement, joy, and vibrance! Become the mad scientist of your brain.

This starts with your new best friend, serotonin: the "happy neurotransmitter." It aids our digestive system, sleep patterns, learning, and relationships.

We often talk about how changing your life starts with changing your thoughts. This is true... But sometimes, it's a bit exhausting to think "happy thoughts," especially if you face real, raw grief and trauma.

To help navigate this, you can reframe your thoughts by starting with your actions.

Because serotonin is connected to our lifestyles, we can take aligned ACTIONS to kick up our serotonin, all-natural! Let's boost your mental health: Pick what speaks to YOU best!

FOOD

Self-care is food (which we'll dive into even more in the final"E" of EMBRACE: Eat Healthily!). Most of our serotonin is processed in our guts. You can't eat serotonin, but you can eat "tryptophan," an amino acid that magically turns into serotonin when combined with carbs.

Some serotonin-boosting combos are:
- Salmon + quinoa or brown rice
- Oatmeal + nuts and berries
- Whole wheat turkey sandwich
- Pineapple + yogurt
- Eggs + toast
- Cheese + nuts (charcuterie board, anyone?)

MOVEMENT

Runner's high is real, as aerobic exercises stimulate blood pumping and serotonin.

Find your favorite way to move, whether walking or hiking in nature, swimming in the pool or ocean, taking an aerobic class, or even dancing around in your kitchen!

SUNLIGHT

Sunshine is Mother Nature's natural medicine. Just 10-15 minutes of pure sunshine elevates our moods and warms our souls.

Remind yourself of the beauty around you with just a few minutes outside each day, whether rainy or cloudy.

MASSAGE

This is your excuse to book the massage. Your body and brain deserve the rejuvenation.

Massages leave our bodies feeling more relaxed and rejuvenated by releasing stress chemicals and pumping up our happy ones.

SLEEP

Take a nap. I mean it!

Sleep is anything but lazy. It sharpens your mind, uplifts your heart, and recharges your body. A 20-minute nap can act as a reset button, while a 10-minute nap can boost your spirits.

Permit yourself to rest –– add a nap to your to-do list.

Journal Prompts

Reflect on a recent day when you experienced a surge of happiness and contentment. What activities or actions were you engaged in during that day?

_____

_____

_____

How can you incorporate more of these activities into your daily life to promote a positive mindset and elevate your serotonin levels naturally?

_____

_____

_____

Explore the connection between your emotions and your lifestyle choices. Are there any habits or behaviors that may be hindering your serotonin production? How can you replace these with healthier, mood-boosting alternatives?

_____

_____

_____

Create a list of activities you've always wanted to try but have not explored. Choose one from the list and commit to trying it within the next week. How does stepping out of your comfort zone and trying something new align with your journey to refuel your soul?

_____

_____

_____

Remember, you have the power to rewire and rejuvenate your brain through intentional actions and lifestyle choices. Embrace the journey of becoming the mad scientist of your brain and fuel your soul for a transformative and uplifting experience!

Exercise

Choose one of the five serotonin-boosting activities and do it!

Eat serotonin-supportive foods!

Move your body in a fun, refreshing way!

Get some sunlight!

Book a massage!

Take a nap!

Exploring New, High–Vibe Routes of Rejuvenation

OBJECTIVE:

To explore your not-so-typical kinds of
rejuvenation to open your mind, body, and
spirit to next-level healing.

A Note of Love:
Your Next Level is on a Whole New Level!

Remember: To leap into your next level, you've got to make next-level moves. You know that next-level version of you —— your higher self.

Sometimes, you've just got to ask yourself, "What would my higher self do?"

Doing that one thing and taking that trip can shift your reality and give you your power back. But continually exploring new, high-vibe routes of rejuvenation can constantly put you in place to RECEIVE your healing.

New experiences open your heart, mind, and soul to the Universe to receive more. It's not just about raising vibrations but showing yourself that you can try new things.

It proves to you that healing isn't linear. No two paths look the same. (and thank goodness for that!)

So today, I want you to do something different. Something out of the box. Depending on who you are, it might be as simple as going out on a Tuesday or staying in on a Friday.

Do something new for yourself! Imagine what the most aligned, high-vibe version of you would do today —— and do it with her.

Journal Prompts

Take a moment to connect with your higher self, the version of you that embodies confidence and alignment. Ask yourself, "What does my higher self truly desire now?" Listen to the whispers of your intuition and write down any insights or inspirations that come to mind.

_____

_____

_____

Reflect on a time when you tried something new or stepped outside of your comfort zone. How did that experience make you feel? What did you learn about yourself in the process? How can you use this knowledge to continue exploring new, high-vibe routes of rejuvenation in your life?

_____

_____

_____

Visualize yourself spending a day with your higher self, engaging in activities that bring joy, fulfillment, and healing. Write a detailed journal entry describing this day, from morning to evening. How does immersing yourself in the energy of your higher self impact your overall well-being and sense of empowerment?

_____

_____

_____

Exercise

Plan and execute a "High-Vibe Day" for yourself.

- Choose a day of the week that feels significant, or pick a day that works for you. Fill your day with activities that resonate with your higher self's desires and aspirations. It could be trying a new hobby, visiting a place you've never been, indulging in self-care rituals, or spending time in nature.

- Throughout the day, be mindful of how each experience makes you feel and its impact on your emotional state. At the end of the day, journal about your "High-Vibe Day" experience and any insights you gained from embodying your higher self's energy.

- Embrace the magic of trying something different and allow yourself to receive the healing and transformation that comes with stepping into your next-level self.

A Note of Love:
Exploring High-Frequency Ways to Hit 'Refresh'

Rejuvenation is the soul's refresh option. Let's hit the refresh button in a new way today!

Woooo weeee! We've discussed everyday self-care moves, like naps, walks, massages, and sunshine. Now, let's think out of the box, give our healing journeys, and use high-vibe healing methods to give our healing journeys the transformative transformation we seek. Let's examine a few of my favorites:

Hyperbaric Chambers

Our bodies heal themselves. Sometimes, we're left with scars that remind us of what we've overcome. They tie us to our past while letting us move forward with our wounds.

Our bodies use oxygen to heal our wounds. It moves and flows through our blood, carrying it to areas needing healing. Oxygen has intuitive, adaptable energy (like our air element friends)! It's the same with mental, emotional, and spiritual wounds.

Hyperbaric Chambers ramp up this healing by increasing the oxygen given to your body, giving the energy needed for our tissue and cells to recover faster. Spending time in a hyperbaric chamber can rejuvenate your mind and body with the dynamic healing energy it needs.

Blood-Spinning Machine

We're still thinking out of the park, so stick with me! Blood spinning (or PRP therapy) injects your healing powers back into your own body.

A practitioner will take a sample of your blood and put it in a centrifuge that separates it into components. They'll inject your platelet-rich plasma into an area that needs healing to concentrate your recovery, helping your body heal.

IV Drips

Your body's healing energy runs through your veins. But sometimes, this energy gets stuck. Blocked. Deprived of what it needs to flow and rejuvenate.

If you've neglected your body for some time, you might consider IV drips. You can inject healing into your bloodstream, quickly delivering healing and nutrients through your veins!

There are drips for hydration, immunity, energy, recovery, and restoration!

Infrared Red Saunas

Trauma can send our souls off-balance. This misalignment of our yin and yang is deeply tied to our bodies' temperature. Yang is your fire energy, centered on action, movement, and growth. Yin is your cold, damp point centered on rest and restoration. When either depleted or overextended, we need to refine our balance.

Infrared saunas can ignite our yang energy, boosting our serotonin, reducing stress, and empowering focus and strength.

Pay attention to the energy you need. What needs to be balanced? Major life events can shift us from alignment, making us feel less and less like ourselves. But tuning into our needs -- focusing on how we can care for ourselves -- leads us back to our center.

Take a giant, rejuvenating leap toward your aligned, higher self today!

Journal Prompts

What HYPER WELLNESS service would you include to align with your higher self's desires and aspirations?

_____

_____

_____

Write a detailed itinerary for this special day, outlining each experience you plan to indulge in.

_____

_____

_____

How do these experiences resonate with your soul? How do you expect each activity to impact your emotional state and overall well-being?

_____

_____

_____

On your "High-Vibe Day," be present and mindful. Take note of changes in your energy, mood, and perspective. Afterward, write down your experiences and insights gained on this healing journey.

_____

_____

_____

Exercise

- Create a "High-Vibe Healing Menu" for yourself, featuring a variety of out-of-the-box healing methods and activities.
- Include options like trying a new holistic therapy, exploring sound healing, journaling with affirmations, meditating in nature, or practicing breathwork exercises.
- Over the next week, experiment with different items from your menu and keep a healing journal to document your experiences, emotions, and any profound shifts you notice.
- At the end of the week, reflect on how these high-vibe healing methods have impacted your overall well-being and rejuvenation journey.
- Embrace the transformative power of trying something new and invite in the magic of healing on a deeper level.

Your Journey, Our Gratitude

Healing doesn't reside in the ceaseless whirlwind of daily life; it finds its home in moments of stillness.

Whether in quiet reflection or much-needed naps, the path to your well-being has already been laid out by your own hands. Now, the compass is in your grasp: your next destination is entirely your call.

Are you content to linger where you are, finding solace in rest and rejuvenation? That's absolutely okay.

Do you feel compelled to move, charting new landscapes of self-discovery? Equally valid.

Healing doesn't adhere to a straight line. It zigzags, it loops, it retraces its steps and then surges forward anew. It's a web of complexity, but it's within that intricate maze that we form a truce with our grief.

Remember that self-care isn't a luxury; it's your right. It's your way of inscribing grief within your narrative of triumph, honoring not just those we've lost but also celebrating the one who remains—you. So go on, extend to yourself the grace of healing and the gift of joy; if anyone is deserving of it, it's you.

With Infinite Intention

The Grief Warrior

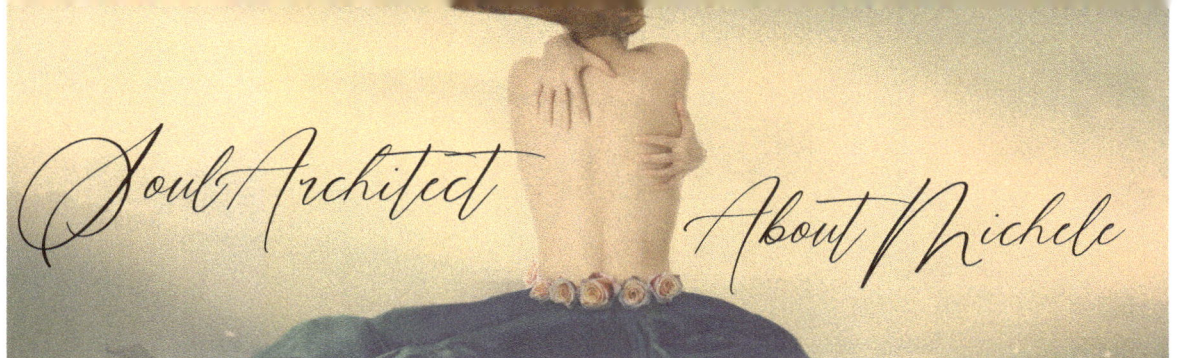

Michele C. Bell's narrative is a profound testament to resilience, the transformative power of embracing life's most profound challenges, and the depth of human compassion. Her journey, which began with the deeply personal and original work "*A Journey of Unconditional Love*," evolved into the 22-time award-winning story, "*A Son's Gift*," marking the inception of her distinguished career as an empathetic voice within the realm of grief literature.

With a Ph.D. in Philosophy and Metaphysics, Michele brings a unique blend of intuitive insight and scholarly depth to "*The 7 Stages of Grief* - **EMBRACE**." This work, unlike traditional grief literature, opens a space where healing is interwoven with personal growth and transformation, guided by Michele's own experiences, her profound journey through PTSD, and her scholarly insights. This journey has not only deepened her understanding of grief and resilience but also infused her writing with authenticity and compassion, offering solace and a transformative roadmap to those navigating the intricacies of loss.

Her innovative approach, blending the profound depths of intuitive philosophy with avant-garde grief counseling modalities, pioneers a novel paradigm in grief literature. Michele's work, transcending meticulous writing and exploration, charts a path towards transformative healing. Each stage, encapsulated within the evocative acronym **EMBRACE**, is meticulously crafted to guide the bereaved with dignity, offering nuanced understanding through the labyrinth of loss.

Beyond her literary contributions, Michele's life story—marked by resilience amidst adversity—enriches her professional narrative. From facing challenges such as bullying and domestic abuse to navigating the complexities of being a holistic real estate broker, Michele's experiences underscore her innate desire to support individuals through significant life transitions. The profound loss of her son to Ewings Sarcoma tested her resolve, catalyzing a shift towards mental health advocacy and the development of groundbreaking methodologies like the Soul Design technique and the *7 Stages of Grief* workbooks.

Michele's contributions extend to her active involvement in suicide prevention and domestic abuse programs, where her voice has become a force for change. Her purpose, whether as a holistic real estate broker, end-of-life expert, or mental health advocate, remains consistent—to support, guide, and uplift. As a member and keynote speaker for the **Daughters of Penelope**, Michele shares inspiring messages of healing, humor, and love, emphasizing the necessity of such virtues in today's world.

At 58, Michele C. Bell, The Grief Warrior®, stands as a testament to the enduring power of the human spirit, commanding respect and fostering deep, authentic connections. Her life experiences, granting her the invaluable CAT credentials of **Compassion, Authenticity, and Trust**, continue to inspire those fortunate enough to encounter her work.

Testimonial

I have been blessed to know Michele—a woman of unshakable spirit, dignity, and beauty.

In facing life's formidable challenges, Michele has crafted a world resplendent with beauty and resilience. Her path, marked by the single-handed upbringing of her children, has been interwoven with a profound dedication to healing and inspiring others. This journey transcends the traditional confines of a career, embodying instead a vocation pursued with unmatched passion and purpose. Her creativity is limitless, merging effortlessly with an intuitive wisdom that has provided solace and direction to many.

Michele's commitment to imparting her knowledge and energy elevates her contributions far beyond the ordinary, rendering her teachings a treasure for those seeking enlightenment and transformative change. Her loyalty to the upliftment of others is profound, positioning her as an invaluable guide for anyone navigating the intricacies of life and seeking healing. I wholeheartedly endorse Michele's works and teachings to anyone drawn to a journey of significant, soulful discovery—her influence is a remarkable gift to the world, unparalleled in its depth and scope.

-JULIAN LAMPERT, CLASSICAL PIANIST

DISCLAIMER

All content within the 7 Stages of Grief Alignment Workbook is original and intended solely to promote mind, body, and spirit well-being. This material does not replace· the expertise or advice of a licensed mental health professional. Grief experiences are unique to each individual, and while the workbook provides supportive tools and perspectives, it does not guarantee specific outcomes. If you are experiencing intense or extreme distress, please consult a professional.

By using this course, you acknowledge and accept these terms and conditions. The 7 Stages of Grief certification program, conceived and developed by Dr. Michele Bell, offers an innovative, holistic, and empathy-driven approach to understanding and navigating grief. It is rooted in comprehensive research and deep insight into the human experience of loss and recovery.

Program Overview:
- Embracing Growth in Grief: Recognize the transformative potential within grief.
- The 7 Stages of Grief: Explore the intricate emotional journey of grief, encompassing its multifaceted seven stages.
- Pivoting with Purpose: Equip yourself with practical tools to channel grief's raw energy into purposeful action.
- Understanding the Power of Resistance: Gain insights into the obstacles resistance can pose on the healing journey and learn strategies to address and overcome it.
- Coping Modalities: Discover and apply various coping methods tailored to individual grief journeys or to assist others on this path.
- Certification: As a culmination, the program offers a certification examination to ensure a comprehensive understanding of the 7 Stages of Grief methodology.

Engage with the 7 Stages of Grief, All-In-One Master Compilation program to acquire a compassionate and informed approach to navigating the intricate labyrinth of grief, whether for personal growth or as a professional commitment.

Remember, every voice matters in bringing light to the shadows of grief. By uniting, we can raise awareness and create a world where everyone feels understood and supported during their moments of profound loss. I deeply appreciate your commitment to this cause. Please take a moment to sign the **Loss Awareness Day** petition on **Change.org**, inspired by the heartfelt endeavors of Lisa Marie Presley. Together, we can make a difference.
With heartfelt gratitude and hope,
MiMi + The Grief Warrior®